Responsible Choices, Stronger Families: The Role of Values in Sustainable Consumption

Johanna

TABLE OF CONTENTS

Chapter 1: Introduction

Background of sustainable consumption and responsible choices

In today's rapidly changing world, the concept of sustainable consumption and responsible choices has gained significant attention. As our planet faces unprecedented environmental challenges, it has become crucial for individuals and families to adopt a conscious and thoughtful approach towards their consumption patterns. This subchapter aims to provide a comprehensive background on sustainable consumption and emphasize the role of family values in making responsible choices.

Sustainable consumption refers to the practice of using resources in a way that meets present needs without compromising the ability of future generations to meet their own needs. It encompasses various aspects of our daily lives, including the products we buy, the food we eat, the energy we use, and the waste we generate. By adopting sustainable consumption practices, we can minimize our ecological footprint, reduce waste, conserve resources, and contribute to a healthier planet.

The importance of family values cannot be understated when discussing sustainable consumption. Family values serve as a moral compass that guides individuals towards responsible choices. Within the context of sustainable consumption, family values play a crucial role in shaping attitudes, behaviors, and decision-making processes. By instilling values such as empathy, respect for nature, and responsibility towards future generations, families can create a strong foundation for sustainable living.

Moreover, responsible choices are not just limited to environmental considerations. They also encompass social and economic dimensions. Making responsible choices means considering the impact of our actions on the well-being of others, both within our communities and globally. It means supporting fair trade, ethical business practices, and social justice initiatives. Responsible choices are about making informed decisions that align with our values and contribute to the greater good.

This subchapter will explore the various factors that influence sustainable consumption and responsible choices. It will delve into the role of education, media, and societal norms in shaping our consumption patterns. Additionally, it will highlight the benefits of adopting sustainable lifestyles, including improved health, financial savings, and a sense of fulfillment and purpose.

By understanding the background of sustainable consumption and the importance of family values, individuals from all walks of life can empower themselves to make responsible choices. This subchapter aims to inspire and educate readers about the transformative potential of sustainable consumption and the instrumental role of family values in creating a better future for ourselves and future generations.

Importance of family values in shaping consumption patterns

In today's fast-paced and consumer-driven world, it is crucial to understand the significant role that family values play in shaping our consumption patterns. Our values serve as a compass, guiding us in making responsible choices and ensuring the sustainability of our consumption habits. This subchapter delves into the importance of family values and how they influence our decision-making process, ultimately leading to a more sustainable and fulfilling lifestyle.

Family values are the principles and beliefs that a family holds dear. They are passed down from one generation to another and form the foundation of our behavior and choices. These values shape our attitudes towards material possessions, money, and the environment. By instilling strong family values, we cultivate a mindset that prioritizes sustainable consumption over excessive consumerism.

One of the primary reasons family values are crucial in shaping consumption patterns is their ability to foster a sense of responsibility. When we prioritize family values, we recognize the impact of our choices on our loved ones and the world around us. We become conscious consumers, considering the long-term consequences of our actions. By prioritizing sustainability and mindful consumption, we can ensure a better future for our families and the planet.

Family values also help create a sense of identity and purpose. When we understand and embrace our family's values, we develop a strong sense of self and belonging. This connection to our roots influences our consumption patterns, as we strive to make choices that align with our family's values. By incorporating these values into our daily lives, we contribute to a collective effort towards sustainable consumption.

Moreover, family values promote intergenerational learning and communication. By engaging in open discussions about values, we can share knowledge and experiences that shape our consumption patterns. This exchange of ideas fosters understanding and empathy, enabling us to make informed choices that align with our family's values.

Family values also serve as a source of emotional support. They provide a sense of stability and security, which can help prevent impulsive and excessive consumption habits. When we prioritize family relationships and emotional well-being over material possessions, we cultivate a more sustainable and fulfilling lifestyle.

In conclusion, family values play a crucial role in shaping our consumption patterns. By prioritizing sustainability, responsibility, and mindful consumption, we can create a better future for our families and the planet. By instilling and embracing these values, we establish a strong foundation for sustainable living that benefits not only ourselves but also future generations. It is essential for us all, regardless of our backgrounds or interests, to recognize the importance of family values in shaping our consumption patterns and work towards a more sustainable and fulfilling lifestyle.

Purpose and scope of the book

The book "Responsible Choices, Stronger Families: The Role of Values in Sustainable Consumption" is an insightful guide that delves into the importance of family values and their impact on sustainable consumption. In a world driven by materialistic desires and rampant consumerism, this book aims to highlight the significance of instilling strong values within families to create a more sustainable and harmonious society.

The purpose of this book is to emphasize the crucial role that family values play in shaping our consumption patterns and overall well-being. It explores how our choices as individuals and families have far-reaching consequences on the environment, economy, and social fabric of our communities. By understanding the significance of values such as empathy, compassion, and responsible decision-making, readers will learn how to make more mindful choices that benefit both their families and the planet.

This book addresses a wide audience, welcoming everyone who is interested in fostering a better understanding of sustainable consumption and its connection to family values. Whether you are a parent seeking ways to instill these values in your children, a young adult starting a family, or someone interested in learning about the impact of values on consumption, this book offers valuable insights and actionable strategies.

Furthermore, this book caters to the niche audience concerned with the importance of family values. It explores how strong family values can serve as a foundation for sustainable consumption practices and create a positive impact on the world. By examining various case studies, expert opinions, and real-life examples, readers will be inspired to reflect on their own values and how they can align them with their consumer choices.

In conclusion, "Responsible Choices, Stronger Families: The Role of Values in Sustainable Consumption" is a comprehensive guide that explores the purpose and scope of family values in relation to sustainable consumption. By reading this book, every individual can gain a deeper understanding of the impact their choices have on the world and learn how to make responsible decisions that contribute to the well-being of their families and the global community.

Chapter 2: Understanding Sustainable Consumption

Definition and concept of sustainable consumption

Sustainable consumption is a term that has gained significant attention in recent years as our society grapples with the urgent need to address environmental challenges. It refers to the consumption of goods and services in a way that meets the needs of the present generation without compromising the ability of future generations to meet their own needs. In simpler terms, it means making responsible choices in our consumption patterns to ensure the long-term well-being of our planet.

At its core, sustainable consumption is about finding a balance between our needs and the Earth's limited resources. It involves considering the environmental, social, and economic impacts of our choices, and striving to minimize harm while maximizing benefits. This concept encourages us to think beyond our immediate desires and consider the long-term consequences of our actions.

Sustainable consumption goes beyond individual actions; it also encompasses the systems and structures that shape our consumption patterns. It involves advocating for policies that promote sustainability, supporting companies that prioritize environmental and social responsibility, and being mindful of the entire lifecycle of a product – from its production to its disposal.

When we talk about sustainable consumption within the context of family values, it becomes even more significant. The family unit plays a crucial role in shaping our values and behaviors, and it is within this unit that we can instill the importance of sustainable consumption. By teaching our children about the impact of their choices on the environment and future generations, we empower them to make responsible decisions from an early age.

Family values, such as empathy, compassion, and responsibility, can serve as a foundation for sustainable consumption. When we prioritize these values, we are more likely to consider the welfare of others and the planet when making consumption choices. By placing importance on these values, we can create a ripple effect that extends beyond our immediate family and influences the wider community.

In conclusion, sustainable consumption entails making conscious choices that take into account the well-being of the planet and future generations. It involves considering the environmental, social, and economic impacts of our consumption patterns. By incorporating family values into our consumption choices, we can create a stronger foundation for sustainable living. It is through responsible choices that we can build a more sustainable future for everyone.

The impact of unsustainable consumption on the environment

Introduction:

In today's fast-paced world, the consequences of unsustainable consumption have become increasingly evident. Our insatiable desire for material possessions, convenience, and instant gratification has taken a toll on the environment, threatening the very ecosystems that sustain life on Earth. This subchapter explores the profound impact of unsustainable consumption on the environment and emphasizes how family values play a crucial role in transitioning towards sustainable choices.

The environmental consequences: Unsustainable consumption patterns have led to the depletion of natural resources, deforestation, pollution, and climate change. Our voracious appetite for goods, from clothing to electronics, has resulted in the extraction of finite resources, often irresponsibly. The production, transportation, and disposal of these goods contribute to greenhouse gas emissions, air and water pollution, and waste accumulation, causing irreversible damage to our planet.

The importance of family values: Family values serve as the foundation upon which sustainable consumption can be built. By instilling values such as empathy, responsibility, and mindfulness in our children, we can shape their understanding of the impact their choices have on the environment. By promoting a sense of interconnectedness with nature and emphasizing the importance of preserving it for future generations, we can create a profound shift towards sustainable lifestyles.

Promoting conscious consumption: Through education and awareness, families can make informed choices about the products they purchase and their impact on the environment. By opting for eco-friendly alternatives, reducing waste, and supporting local and sustainable businesses, we can contribute to the preservation of our planet's resources. Teaching children about the consequences of their actions and involving them in sustainable practices from a young age can empower them to become conscious consumers and responsible stewards of the environment.

The power of collective action: Recognizing that the challenge of unsustainable consumption is not an individual one, but a collective responsibility, is essential. Families can join community initiatives, participate in environmental campaigns, and advocate for policies that support sustainability. By working together, we can amplify our impact and create a greener, more sustainable future for all.

Conclusion:
The impact of unsustainable consumption on the environment is undeniable, but with the right values and conscious choices, we can mitigate its effects. By embracing family values that prioritize sustainability, we can foster a generation that values the environment and takes responsibility for their actions. Together, we can make a significant difference, protecting the planet for future generations and ensuring a brighter future for all.

Current trends and challenges in sustainable consumption

In today's fast-paced world, sustainable consumption has become an increasingly important topic for individuals, families, and communities. As we strive to create a more sustainable future, it is essential to understand the current trends and challenges that surround this concept.

One of the major trends in sustainable consumption is a shift towards conscious consumerism. People are becoming more aware of the impact their choices have on the environment and are actively seeking out sustainable alternatives. From clothing and food to energy and transportation, individuals are making responsible choices that align with their values.

Another trend is the rise of the sharing economy. Collaborative consumption, as it is often referred to, allows individuals to share resources, reducing waste and maximizing efficiency. This trend has given birth to platforms like car-sharing services, co-working spaces, and community gardens, enabling people to access goods and services without the need for excessive ownership.

However, along with these positive trends, there are also challenges that need to be addressed. One of the main challenges is the lack of awareness and education surrounding sustainable consumption. Many individuals are simply not aware of the environmental and social impacts of their choices. Therefore, it is crucial to raise awareness and provide education on the importance of sustainable consumption, particularly within the family unit.

Family values play a significant role in shaping sustainable consumption habits. By instilling values such as responsibility, empathy, and environmental consciousness in children, families can contribute to a more sustainable future. Teaching children to appreciate and care for the environment, to understand the consequences of their actions, and to prioritize sustainable choices will have a lasting impact on their consumption habits as they grow older.

Another challenge is the affordability and accessibility of sustainable products and services. While the demand for sustainable alternatives is increasing, many individuals face financial constraints that limit their ability to make sustainable choices. Governments, businesses, and communities need to work together to make sustainable options more affordable and accessible to everyone.

Overcoming these challenges requires collective action. Governments can implement policies that incentivize sustainable practices, businesses can invest in sustainable technologies, and communities can come together to create shared resources and support networks.

In conclusion, current trends in sustainable consumption show a positive shift towards more responsible choices. However, challenges such as lack of awareness and accessibility need to be addressed. By promoting family values that prioritize sustainability and working together as a society, we can create a future where sustainable consumption is the norm, benefiting not only the environment but also our families and communities.

Chapter 3: The Role of Family Values in Consumption Patterns

The influence of family values on individual choices

Family values play a crucial role in shaping our individual choices and actions. In a world where consumption patterns are driven by materialism and instant gratification, it is essential to recognize the importance of family values in promoting sustainable consumption and responsible choices. This subchapter aims to explore the significant influence that family values have on our decision-making process and how they contribute to building stronger families and a more sustainable future.

Family values serve as a foundation for our moral compass. They provide us with a set of guiding principles that shape our beliefs, attitudes, and behaviors. When these values are instilled from a young age, they become deeply ingrained within us, influencing our choices and actions throughout our lives. The importance of family values lies in their ability to foster empathy, compassion, and a sense of responsibility towards ourselves, others, and the environment.

Strong family values encourage us to prioritize long-term well-being over short-term gains. They teach us to make conscious choices that consider the impact on our loved ones, society, and the planet. For instance, a family that values sustainability will likely make choices that prioritize eco-friendly products, reduce waste, and conserve resources. This not only benefits the environment but also sets an example for future generations to follow.

Moreover, family values create a supportive environment that encourages open dialogue and mutual respect. When family members share common values, they can engage in meaningful conversations about responsible consumption, ethics, and sustainability. Such discussions enable individuals to critically evaluate their choices and align them with their family's values. This not only strengthens family bonds but also empowers individuals to make informed decisions that contribute to a more sustainable world.

In conclusion, the influence of family values on individual choices cannot be underestimated. Family values shape our beliefs, attitudes, and behaviors, and guide us towards responsible and sustainable consumption. By instilling strong family values, we can create a ripple effect that extends beyond the household, positively impacting our communities and the planet. It is crucial for every individual to recognize the importance of family values and actively incorporate them into their decision-making process, for only then can we build stronger families and work towards a more sustainable future.

Teaching sustainable consumption through family values

In our fast-paced world, where consumerism has become the norm, it is essential to instill the values of sustainable consumption in our families. This subchapter aims to shed light on the importance of family values in teaching and promoting sustainable consumption practices. By embracing these values, we can create a sustainable future for ourselves, our families, and the planet.

Family values play a crucial role in shaping the mindset and behaviors of individuals, especially in the context of consumption. When parents prioritize sustainable choices and incorporate them into their everyday lives, their children observe and learn from this behavior. By teaching sustainable consumption through family values, we can empower the younger generation to make responsible choices that contribute to a sustainable future.

One of the key family values that can promote sustainable consumption is mindfulness. Encouraging family members to be mindful of their consumption patterns and the impact they have on the environment can lead to more conscious decision-making. This can involve discussing the consequences of excessive consumption, such as resource depletion and pollution, and exploring alternative options that are more sustainable.

Another important family value is gratitude. By cultivating a sense of gratitude for what we have, we can reduce the desire for excessive consumption. Teaching children to appreciate the value of resources and the effort it takes to produce them can help them develop a more sustainable mindset. This can be achieved through activities such as practicing gratitude rituals or engaging in discussions about the importance of valuing what we already possess.

Additionally, fostering empathy within the family can promote sustainable consumption. By encouraging family members to consider the needs of others and the impact of their choices on society, we can develop a sense of responsibility towards the welfare of others and the environment. Engaging in acts of kindness, such as donating unused items or volunteering together as a family, can help instill empathy and a sense of social and environmental responsibility.

Teaching sustainable consumption through family values is not only beneficial for the environment but also for the well-being and unity of the family. By prioritizing sustainable choices and engaging in activities that promote responsible consumption, families can strengthen their bond, create lasting memories, and pave the way for a more sustainable future.

In conclusion, family values play a vital role in teaching and promoting sustainable consumption practices. By incorporating values such as mindfulness, gratitude, and empathy into our daily lives, we can guide our families towards making responsible choices that contribute to a sustainable future. Embracing these values not only benefits the environment but also strengthens family bonds, creating a more harmonious and fulfilling life for everyone.

The intergenerational transmission of values and consumption patterns

The intergenerational transmission of values and consumption patterns is a topic of great importance in today's society. In the book "Responsible Choices, Stronger Families: The Role of Values in Sustainable Consumption," we delve deep into the significance of family values and how they shape our consumption patterns over generations.

Family values are the principles, beliefs, and ideals that are passed down from one generation to another within a family. These values play a crucial role in shaping an individual's behavior, choices, and lifestyle. They influence not only the way we perceive the world but also the way we consume and interact with our environment.

The intergenerational transmission of values occurs when parents pass on their beliefs and attitudes towards consumption to their children. This process is often unconscious and happens through observation, imitation, and direct communication. Children learn not only what to consume but also how to consume it from their parents, which can have a significant impact on their own future choices.

Understanding the intergenerational transmission of values and consumption patterns is essential for everyone because it helps us comprehend the power of family in shaping our attitudes and behaviors towards sustainable consumption. By recognizing the influence of our family values, we can make responsible choices that align with our own beliefs and contribute to a more sustainable future.

Moreover, this knowledge is particularly relevant for those who value the importance of family values. It highlights the role that parents and caregivers play in instilling positive values in their children. By consciously transmitting values that promote sustainable consumption, we can create a ripple effect that extends beyond our immediate family and positively impacts society as a whole.

In conclusion, the intergenerational transmission of values and consumption patterns is a crucial aspect of sustainable consumption. By understanding and embracing the importance of family values, we can make responsible choices that align with our beliefs and contribute to a more sustainable future. Whether you are a parent, a young adult, or simply interested in building a better world, this subchapter will provide valuable insights into the power of family and the role it plays in shaping our consumption patterns.

Chapter 4: Values-Based Decision Making for Sustainable Consumption

Identifying and prioritizing values for sustainable consumption

In today's fast-paced world, where consumerism is at its peak, it is crucial to take a step back and reflect on our consumption patterns. As individuals, we have the power to make responsible choices that can significantly impact our environment and future generations. To achieve this, it is essential to identify and prioritize values that align with sustainable consumption.

Sustainable consumption refers to the practice of using resources in a way that meets our current needs without compromising the ability of future generations to meet their own needs. It requires us to be mindful of our choices and their potential impact on the environment, society, and economy.

Identifying our values is the first step towards sustainable consumption. Values are the guiding principles that shape our behaviors and choices. They are deeply ingrained in our upbringing, culture, and personal beliefs. When it comes to sustainable consumption, family values play a pivotal role.

Family values have always been regarded as the foundation of a cohesive and responsible society. They provide a moral compass that guides our actions and shapes our worldview. By understanding the importance of family values, we can harness their power to drive sustainable consumption practices.

When identifying values for sustainable consumption, it is crucial to prioritize those that promote environmental stewardship, social justice, and economic well-being. Environmental stewardship values encourage us to minimize our ecological footprint, conserve resources, and protect biodiversity. Social justice values promote fair trade, human rights, and inclusivity in our consumption choices. Economic well-being values focus on supporting local economies, ethical business practices, and reducing waste.

By prioritizing these values, we can make conscious decisions in our everyday lives. For example, we can choose to buy products with minimal packaging, support local farmers' markets, opt for fair trade products, and reduce our energy consumption. These actions not only benefit the environment but also contribute to the sustainable development of communities.

In conclusion, identifying and prioritizing values for sustainable consumption is crucial in today's consumer-driven society. By acknowledging the importance of family values and incorporating them into our decision-making process, we can create a positive impact on our environment, society, and economy. It is up to each one of us to make responsible choices that align with our values and ensure a better future for generations to come.

Applying values to everyday choices

In today's fast-paced and consumer-driven world, it can be easy to get caught up in the whirlwind of choices and decisions we face on a daily basis. From what we wear, to what we eat, to how we spend our free time, our lives are filled with countless opportunities to make choices. But have you ever stopped to consider the values that guide these choices?

In this subchapter, titled "Applying Values to Everyday Choices," we delve into the importance of family values and how they can shape our decisions towards sustainable consumption.

Family values are the core principles and beliefs that a family holds dear. They are the moral compass that guides our actions and the foundation upon which strong families are built. By applying these values to our everyday choices, we not only foster a sense of personal responsibility but also contribute to a more sustainable future.

When we make conscious decisions based on our family values, we prioritize what truly matters to us. For example, if environmental stewardship is a value that your family holds dear, you may choose to buy products with minimal packaging, use reusable bags, or reduce energy consumption at home. These small actions, when multiplied by millions of individuals, can have a significant positive impact on the environment.

Furthermore, applying family values to everyday choices helps us align our actions with our beliefs. It allows us to live a more authentic and meaningful life, where our decisions are in harmony with what we hold dear. This sense of congruence brings a deep sense of satisfaction and fulfillment, knowing that our choices are consistent with our values.

In addition to personal satisfaction, applying family values to everyday choices also sets a powerful example for those around us, especially for younger family members. Children learn by observing their parents and caregivers, and when they see their role models making responsible and sustainable choices, they are more likely to embrace these values themselves.

Ultimately, applying family values to everyday choices is a transformative act that goes beyond our personal lives. It has the potential to create a ripple effect, inspiring others to reevaluate their own choices and adopt more sustainable practices. By consciously aligning our actions with our values, we can contribute to a brighter future for ourselves, our families, and generations to come.

In conclusion, the subchapter "Applying Values to Everyday Choices" emphasizes the importance of family values in guiding our decisions towards sustainable consumption. By prioritizing what truly matters to us, aligning our actions with our beliefs, and setting an example for others, we not only improve our own lives but also contribute to a more sustainable and compassionate world. So, let us reflect on our family values and use them as a compass to make responsible choices that will strengthen our families and create a better future for all.

Overcoming barriers to values-based decision making

In today's fast-paced and consumer-driven world, it can be challenging to make decisions that align with our core values. We are constantly bombarded with advertisements and societal pressures that can sway us away from what truly matters to us. However, overcoming these barriers is crucial for maintaining strong family values and leading a sustainable lifestyle.

One of the main barriers to values-based decision making is the influence of external factors. Peer pressure, societal norms, and media messages often push us towards materialism and instant gratification. It can be tempting to succumb to these pressures and make choices that are contrary to our values. However, by being aware of these influences and actively questioning their impact on our decision-making process, we can begin to overcome this barrier.

Another barrier is the lack of awareness about our own values. Many of us have never taken the time to reflect on what truly matters to us and what kind of legacy we want to leave behind. By engaging in self-reflection and open conversations with our loved ones, we can gain a deeper understanding of our values and how they shape our decisions. This awareness will enable us to make choices that are in line with our beliefs and contribute to the well-being of our families and the planet.

Additionally, a lack of education and information about sustainable consumption practices can hinder our ability to make values-based decisions. It is important for everyone to stay informed about the impact of our choices on the environment and society. By seeking out reliable sources of information, attending workshops, or joining community initiatives, we can overcome this barrier and make more responsible choices.

Lastly, fear and resistance to change can also impede values-based decision making. Sometimes, choosing a sustainable lifestyle requires stepping out of our comfort zones and breaking away from familiar habits. However, by embracing change and understanding the positive impact it can have on our families and the world, we can overcome this barrier and make choices that align with our values.

In conclusion, overcoming barriers to values-based decision making is essential for creating a sustainable and fulfilling life for ourselves and our families. By being aware of external influences, understanding our own values, seeking out education and information, and embracing change, we can overcome these barriers and make choices that are in line with our deepest beliefs. Let us remember that our choices matter, and by making responsible decisions, we can create a brighter future for ourselves, our families, and the world we inhabit.

Chapter 5: Nurturing Responsible Consumption through Family Practices

Promoting conscious consumption within the family

In today's fast-paced and consumer-driven world, it is crucial to instill conscious consumption practices within our families. By doing so, we not only contribute to a sustainable future but also strengthen the core values that bind our families together. In this subchapter, we will explore the significance of family values and how they play a pivotal role in promoting responsible choices and sustainable consumption.

Family values serve as a moral compass, guiding us towards making decisions that align with our beliefs and principles. When it comes to consumption, these values can help us prioritize sustainability, mindful purchasing, and reducing waste. By fostering an environment that encourages conscious consumption, we empower each family member to be more mindful of their choices and their impact on the planet.

One effective way to promote conscious consumption within the family is through open and honest communication. Regular discussions about the importance of sustainable living, climate change, and the consequences of overconsumption can help raise awareness and build a collective understanding. Engaging in such conversations allows family members to share their thoughts, ideas, and concerns, ultimately strengthening their commitment to responsible choices.

Another valuable aspect of promoting conscious consumption within the family is leading by example. Parents, as role models, have a significant influence on children's behavior and attitudes. By demonstrating sustainable practices such as recycling, reducing energy consumption, and supporting local businesses, parents can inspire their children to adopt similar habits. Moreover, involving children in decision-making processes, such as choosing eco-friendly products or planning sustainable family activities, empowers them to take ownership of their choices and develop a sense of responsibility towards the environment.

Creating a family culture that values experiences over material possessions also fosters conscious consumption. Encouraging activities such as hiking, gardening, cooking meals together, or volunteering as a family not only strengthens bonds but also reduces the desire for excessive consumption. By shifting the focus from material goods to shared experiences, families can create lasting memories while minimizing their ecological footprint.

In conclusion, promoting conscious consumption within the family is essential for building stronger family values and contributing to a sustainable future. By engaging in open conversations, leading by example, and prioritizing experiences over material possessions, families can instill the importance of responsible choices in each family member. These values will not only benefit the planet but also strengthen the bond between family members, fostering a sense of unity and shared responsibility for a better world.

Encouraging sustainable lifestyles through family rituals

Family rituals play a significant role in shaping the values and behaviors of individuals. These rituals, when infused with a focus on sustainable living, have the potential to create lasting positive impacts on both the environment and the family unit itself. In this subchapter, we delve into the importance of family values and how they can be harnessed to encourage sustainable lifestyles.

Family values serve as the foundation for the development of individuals within a household and can significantly influence their choices and actions. By instilling sustainable values, families can create a culture of environmental consciousness that extends beyond individual behaviors. This subchapter explores the ways in which family rituals can be leveraged to foster sustainable living practices and promote a sense of responsibility towards the planet.

Family meals, for instance, are a prime opportunity to promote sustainable food choices and reduce food waste. By involving children in meal planning, grocery shopping, and cooking, families can educate their younger members about the importance of opting for locally sourced, organic, and seasonal produce. Moreover, adopting habits such as composting and recycling can be a part of the family routine, thus ingraining sustainable practices into everyday life.

Another important aspect of family rituals is the celebration of special occasions. Birthdays, anniversaries, and holidays can be transformed into opportunities to emphasize sustainability. Families can engage in eco-friendly gift exchanges, encourage homemade presents, or support local artisans. Furthermore, organizing nature-based activities, such as hiking, camping, or gardening, can help create a stronger connection between the family and the environment, fostering a love and appreciation for nature.

In addition, family rituals that involve volunteering and community engagement can instill a sense of responsibility towards society and the environment. Families can participate in local cleanup drives, tree planting events, or conservation projects, creating lasting memories and a shared commitment to sustainable practices.

Encouraging sustainable lifestyles through family rituals is not only beneficial for the environment but also strengthens family bonds and instills important values in younger generations. By incorporating sustainability into daily routines and special occasions, families can collectively create a positive impact on the planet and inspire others to follow suit.

In conclusion, family rituals provide a unique opportunity to promote sustainable living practices and values. By infusing these rituals with a focus on environmental consciousness, families can encourage sustainable choices and behaviors. The importance of family values cannot be underestimated, as they shape individuals and their attitudes towards the world. By incorporating sustainable practices into family routines, celebrations, and community engagement, families can build a stronger sense of responsibility towards the planet and create a lasting legacy of sustainability for future generations.

Teaching children about responsible consumption through family activities

In today's consumer-driven society, it is crucial to instill in our children the values of responsible consumption from an early age. By teaching them about the impact of their choices and actions on the environment and society, we can empower them to make responsible choices that will contribute to a sustainable future. One effective way to achieve this is through engaging family activities that not only educate children but also foster a sense of togetherness and shared responsibility.

Family activities provide a unique opportunity to create lasting memories while teaching children about responsible consumption. By involving children in activities such as gardening, cooking, or even shopping, parents can impart important lessons about sustainability and conscious decision-making. For example, growing a vegetable garden together teaches children about the value of locally sourced, organic produce, reducing food waste, and the joy of self-sufficiency. Similarly, involving children in meal planning and preparation can help them understand the importance of choosing healthy, sustainable ingredients and minimizing packaging waste.

Engaging children in shopping activities can also be a valuable teaching moment. By discussing the environmental and social impacts of different products, parents can guide their children towards more responsible choices. Explaining concepts such as fair trade, organic certification, and eco-friendly packaging can help children develop a critical mindset when making purchasing decisions. Moreover, involving children in budgeting and financial planning discussions can foster a sense of responsibility and encourage them to prioritize needs over wants.

Beyond specific activities, it is crucial to cultivate a culture of responsible consumption within the family. By setting an example through our own actions, we can inspire our children to follow suit. For instance, reducing waste by recycling, reusing, and repairing items instead of buying new ones not only saves money but also teaches children the importance of resourcefulness and environmental stewardship.

In conclusion, teaching children about responsible consumption through family activities is an effective way to instill values of sustainability and conscious decision-making from an early age. By engaging children in gardening, cooking, shopping, and other activities, parents can educate them about the environmental and social impacts of their choices. Moreover, fostering a culture of responsible consumption within the family through setting an example and prioritizing sustainable practices will help children develop a lifelong commitment to making responsible choices. By equipping our children with these values, we are not only strengthening our families but also contributing to a more sustainable and just future for all.

Chapter 6: The Impact of Family Values on Sustainable Consumption

Case studies highlighting the role of family values in sustainable consumption

Introduction:

In today's fast-paced world, sustainable consumption is becoming more crucial than ever. It is not just a choice but a responsibility that each individual must embrace. The importance of family values cannot be overstated when it comes to fostering sustainable consumption habits. This subchapter aims to present case studies that illustrate how family values play a pivotal role in promoting sustainable consumption. By examining real-life examples, we hope to inspire and encourage every individual to embrace these values and contribute to a more sustainable future.

Case Study 1: The Johnson Family
The Johnson family, based in a small suburban town, set out on a mission to reduce their carbon footprint. They implemented several sustainable practices, such as switching to renewable energy sources, growing their own organic vegetables, and minimizing food waste. The driving force behind their success was their strong family values of environmental stewardship and responsibility. By involving their children in these activities, the Johnsons instilled a sense of purpose and commitment towards sustainable consumption, ensuring that these values will be carried forward to future generations.

Case Study 2: The Patel Family
The Patel family, residing in a bustling city, recognized the detrimental

impact of excessive consumerism on the environment. They embraced the value of conscious consumption and made a conscious effort to reduce their materialistic tendencies. By adopting a minimalist lifestyle, the Patels focused on quality over quantity and sought out sustainable alternatives for their daily needs. This shift in mindset not only made them happier and more content as a family but also reduced their ecological footprint significantly.

Case Study 3: The Garcia Family

The Garcia family, with their diverse cultural background, prioritized the value of intergenerational knowledge and community engagement. They drew inspiration from their ancestors' traditional practices and integrated them into their modern lives. By reviving practices such as composting, using natural remedies, and repurposing items, the Garcias demonstrated the power of family values in preserving cultural heritage and promoting sustainable consumption. Their efforts not only benefited the environment but also fostered a stronger sense of identity and connection within the family.

Conclusion:

These case studies highlight the transformative power of family values in promoting sustainable consumption. Whether it is a commitment to environmental stewardship, conscious consumption, or preserving cultural heritage, family values act as a guiding force that shapes our choices and behaviors. By embracing these values, every individual has the potential to contribute to a more sustainable future. It is within our collective responsibility to nurture and uphold these values, ensuring a better world for future generations.

Success stories of families adopting sustainable lifestyles

In the pursuit of a more sustainable future, families play a crucial role. By adopting sustainable lifestyles, these families are not only making responsible choices but also empowering themselves to create a positive impact on the environment and society. Here, we delve into the success stories of families who have embraced sustainable consumption, highlighting their inspiring journeys and underscoring the importance of family values in this transformative process.

Meet the Johnsons, a tight-knit family of four that embarked on a mission to reduce their carbon footprint. They started by making small changes such as using energy-efficient appliances and turning off lights when not in use. As their commitment grew, they further integrated sustainable practices into their daily lives. They began growing their own organic vegetables, reducing food waste, and opting for eco-friendly transportation methods like cycling or carpooling. Through these efforts, the Johnsons not only significantly decreased their environmental impact but also strengthened their family bond by working together towards a common goal.

Another remarkable success story comes from the Martinez family, who took a holistic approach to sustainable living. They recognized that responsible consumption extended beyond just environmental considerations and included social and economic aspects as well. The Martinez family actively supported local businesses, bought fair-trade products, and engaged in volunteer work within their community. By embracing these values, they not only reduced their ecological footprint but also contributed to the well-being and development of their society.

The stories of the Johnsons and the Martinez family exemplify the transformative power of family values in fostering sustainable consumption. These families understand that their choices today will shape the world their children inherit tomorrow. By instilling values of responsibility, empathy, and mindfulness, they are equipping their children with the tools to become environmentally conscious and socially responsible citizens.

It is crucial for every family to recognize the importance of their values in the adoption of sustainable lifestyles. By prioritizing sustainable consumption, families not only contribute to a healthier planet but also create a stronger family unit. Shared goals and a sense of purpose strengthen the bond between family members and create a supportive environment for change.

In conclusion, success stories of families adopting sustainable lifestyles serve as a powerful inspiration for all of us. They demonstrate that through the adoption of responsible choices and the cultivation of family values, we can create a more sustainable future for generations to come. Let these stories motivate us to embrace sustainable consumption, knowing that our individual efforts, when combined with those of our families, can lead to a more prosperous and harmonious world.

Lessons learned from families practicing responsible choices

In the subchapter "Lessons learned from families practicing responsible choices" of the book "Responsible Choices, Stronger Families: The Role of Values in Sustainable Consumption," we delve into the importance of family values and how they contribute to sustainable consumption. This chapter is intended for a broad audience, as it is relevant to everyone, regardless of their background or lifestyle choices.

Family values are the fundamental principles and beliefs that guide a family's behavior and decision-making process. When these values align with responsible choices and sustainable consumption, they can have a profound impact on both the family and the wider community.

One crucial lesson we can learn from families practicing responsible choices is the importance of mindfulness. By being mindful of their consumption patterns, families can make conscious decisions that are in line with their values. This means considering the social, economic, and environmental impacts of their choices, and striving for a more sustainable lifestyle.

Another lesson is the power of education and awareness. Families that prioritize responsible choices often invest time and effort into educating themselves and their children about the consequences of their actions. By understanding the impact of their consumption habits, families can make informed decisions and become agents of change within their communities.

Communication is also a key lesson we can learn from these families. Open and honest discussions about values and responsible choices help create a shared vision and strengthen family bonds. By involving every family member in decision-making processes, families can foster a sense of ownership and responsibility, leading to more sustainable consumption practices.

Furthermore, families practicing responsible choices often prioritize quality over quantity. They understand that true happiness and fulfillment do not come from material possessions but from experiences, relationships, and personal growth. By shifting their focus towards experiences and investing in long-lasting and sustainable products, these families contribute to a more sustainable future.

Lastly, families that practice responsible choices serve as role models for future generations. By instilling these values in their children, they ensure that the legacy of sustainability and responsible consumption continues. These families teach their children to be mindful consumers, to question societal norms, and to consider the impact of their actions on the planet and future generations.

In conclusion, the subchapter "Lessons learned from families practicing responsible choices" highlights the importance of family values in sustainable consumption. By being mindful, educating themselves, communicating openly, prioritizing quality, and serving as role models, these families contribute to a more sustainable future. Regardless of our background or lifestyle choices, we can all learn from these lessons and make responsible choices that will lead to stronger families and a more sustainable world.

Chapter 7: Strengthening Families through Sustainable Consumption

Building stronger family bonds through shared values

In today's fast-paced and ever-changing world, it is easy to get caught up in the chaos of daily life and lose sight of what truly matters. Our families are our foundation, the support system that keeps us grounded and provides us with love, security, and a sense of belonging. However, in order to build strong and lasting family bonds, it is essential to have shared values that guide our actions and decisions.

Family values are the principles and beliefs that shape the way we live our lives and influence how we interact with one another. They act as a compass, guiding us through the ups and downs of life, and help us navigate the challenges that come our way. When families share common values, it creates a sense of unity and purpose, allowing them to face adversity together and strengthen their bonds.

One of the most important aspects of building stronger family bonds through shared values is the ability to communicate openly and honestly. By engaging in meaningful conversations, we can explore and understand each other's perspectives, allowing us to find common ground and build a foundation of trust. This open communication also enables us to resolve conflicts more effectively, fostering a healthy and supportive environment within the family.

Shared values also play a crucial role in shaping our behaviors and lifestyle choices. When families have a set of shared values, they are more likely to make responsible choices that are in line with these values. For example, if environmental sustainability is a shared value, the family may choose to reduce their carbon footprint by conserving energy, recycling, or using eco-friendly products. Not only does this promote sustainable consumption, but it also teaches children the importance of making conscious choices that have a positive impact on the world around them.

Furthermore, shared values can provide a sense of identity and belonging within the family unit. They create a common language and set of expectations that everyone can align with, fostering a sense of unity and purpose. This shared identity strengthens family bonds by creating a strong support network and providing a sense of security and stability.

In conclusion, building stronger family bonds through shared values is essential for creating a harmonious and sustainable family life. By fostering open communication, making responsible choices, and creating a shared sense of identity, families can create a strong foundation that withstands the test of time. In this fast-paced world, let us not forget the importance of family values and the profound impact they can have on our lives.

Empowering families to make a positive impact on the environment

In today's rapidly changing world, it is becoming increasingly important for families to take an active role in protecting and preserving the environment. By adopting sustainable practices and instilling values that prioritize environmental responsibility, families can make a significant positive impact on the world around them. This subchapter will explore the ways in which families can empower themselves to create a more sustainable future.

One of the key factors in empowering families to make a positive impact on the environment is the importance of family values. By instilling values that prioritize environmental stewardship, families can create a strong foundation for sustainable living. Teaching children the importance of conserving resources, reducing waste, and respecting nature from an early age will help to shape their attitudes and behavior towards the environment as they grow. It is crucial for parents and caregivers to lead by example and demonstrate these values in their own daily lives.

Family activities and projects centered around sustainability can also be a powerful tool for empowering families. Engaging in activities such as community cleanups, composting, or starting a family garden can not only help to reduce the family's environmental impact but also provide valuable opportunities for learning and bonding. By involving every member of the family in these activities, a sense of shared responsibility and purpose can be cultivated.

In addition, empowering families to make a positive impact on the environment involves equipping them with the knowledge and resources necessary to make sustainable choices. Providing information on eco-friendly products, energy-saving practices, and waste reduction techniques can help families make more informed decisions in their daily lives. It is important to highlight that sustainable living doesn't have to be overwhelming or expensive. Simple changes such as using reusable water bottles, reducing single-use plastic, and conserving energy can make a significant difference when adopted collectively by families.

Ultimately, empowering families to make a positive impact on the environment goes beyond individual actions. It is about fostering a collective consciousness and recognizing that the choices we make as families have far-reaching implications for future generations. By embracing sustainable values, engaging in eco-conscious activities, and equipping ourselves with knowledge, families can become powerful agents of change in building a more sustainable and harmonious world for everyone. Together, we have the ability to create a brighter future for our families and the planet we call home.

Creating a sustainable future for generations to come

In today's fast-paced and consumer-driven world, it is more important than ever to reflect on the impact our choices have on the environment and future generations. This subchapter explores the crucial role that family values play in shaping sustainable consumption habits and creating a better world for all.

Family values are the guiding principles that shape the behavior and decisions of individuals within a family unit. They are the foundation upon which sustainable practices can be built. By instilling values such as environmental consciousness, empathy, and responsibility in our children, we can ensure that they grow up to become conscientious consumers who prioritize the health of the planet and the well-being of future generations.

One of the key aspects of creating a sustainable future lies in cultivating an appreciation for the natural world within our families. By spending time outdoors, engaging in activities that promote environmental stewardship, and educating our children about the importance of biodiversity and ecological balance, we can foster a deep connection with nature. This connection will inspire a sense of responsibility towards preserving the planet and motivate sustainable choices in our everyday lives.

Another essential value to instill in our families is empathy. By teaching our children to consider the needs and perspectives of others, we cultivate a mindset of compassion and cooperation. This mindset is crucial when it comes to sustainable consumption, as it encourages us to think beyond our immediate desires and consider the long-term consequences of our actions. By prioritizing the well-being of others and future generations, we can make more responsible choices that minimize waste, reduce carbon emissions, and promote social and economic equality.

Responsibility is also a fundamental family value that plays a vital role in sustainable consumption. By teaching our children the importance of taking responsibility for their actions, we empower them to make conscious decisions that align with their values. This means understanding the impact of our choices on the environment, seeking out sustainable alternatives, and holding ourselves accountable for the environmental footprint we leave behind.

Creating a sustainable future for generations to come requires collective effort and individual commitment. By embracing family values that prioritize environmental consciousness, empathy, and responsibility, we can lay the groundwork for a more sustainable and equitable world. It is up to each one of us to make responsible choices that not only strengthen our families but also protect the planet for future generations. Together, we can create a legacy of sustainable consumption that will leave a positive and lasting impact on the world.

Chapter 8: Conclusion

Recap of key points discussed in the book

In the book "Responsible Choices, Stronger Families: The Role of Values in Sustainable Consumption," we have explored the significance of family values and their impact on sustainable consumption. Throughout the chapters, we have delved into various aspects of this crucial topic, highlighting the importance of fostering strong family values for a more sustainable future. Let's recap the key points discussed and their relevance to everyone, regardless of their background or beliefs.

Firstly, we emphasized the role of family values as the foundation for responsible consumption. By instilling values such as empathy, compassion, and mindfulness within our families, we can develop a collective consciousness towards sustainable choices. Recognizing the interconnectedness of our actions and their broader consequences is essential for building a more sustainable world.

Secondly, the book underlined the significance of communication within families. Open and honest conversations about values and responsible consumption create an environment where individuals can share their perspectives and learn from one another. These dialogues enable us to collectively develop a set of shared values that guide our consumption patterns and promote sustainable living.

Another key point discussed was the importance of education and awareness. By educating ourselves and our families about the environmental, social, and economic impacts of our choices, we can make more informed decisions. This knowledge empowers us to seek sustainable alternatives, reduce our ecological footprint, and support ethical practices.

Furthermore, the book emphasized the value of leading by example. As parents, caregivers, or influential figures within our families, our actions carry significant weight. By embodying the values we wish to instill in our loved ones, we inspire and motivate them to follow suit. Our collective efforts towards sustainable consumption can create a ripple effect, positively influencing our communities and society as a whole.

Lastly, the book touched upon the importance of resilience and adaptability. In a rapidly changing world, it is crucial to embrace flexibility and adjust our consumption patterns accordingly. By being open to new ideas and approaches, we can navigate the complexities of sustainable living and make responsible choices that align with our values.

In conclusion, "Responsible Choices, Stronger Families: The Role of Values in Sustainable Consumption" has shed light on the significance of family values in promoting sustainable consumption. By fostering open communication, education, leadership, resilience, and adaptability within our families, we can collectively contribute to a more sustainable future. Regardless of our backgrounds or beliefs, the principles explored in this book are relevant to everyone as we strive to create a better world for future generations.

The importance of valuing responsible choices for stronger families

In today's fast-paced and consumer-driven world, it is more crucial than ever to recognize the significance of responsible choices in strengthening our families. Families are the building blocks of society, and the values we instill within them have a profound impact on the well-being and sustainability of our communities. This subchapter aims to shed light on the importance of family values and how valuing responsible choices can lead to stronger, more resilient families.

Family values are the guiding principles that shape our behaviors, attitudes, and interactions within the family unit. They provide a moral compass for each family member and establish a foundation of trust, respect, and empathy. By placing a high value on responsible choices, families can foster a sense of accountability and mindfulness toward their actions and their impact on the world around them.

Responsible choices encompass a wide range of behaviors, including sustainable consumption, ethical decision-making, and conscious parenting. By consciously choosing to live in a more sustainable and environmentally-friendly manner, families can contribute to the preservation of our planet for future generations. This can be achieved through practices such as reducing waste, conserving energy, and supporting eco-friendly products and services.

Ethical decision-making involves considering the consequences of our choices on others and the environment. By teaching our children the importance of empathy, fairness, and social responsibility, we equip them with the tools to make responsible choices that positively impact those around them. This, in turn, strengthens the bonds within the family and cultivates a sense of belonging and harmony.

Conscious parenting is another crucial aspect of valuing responsible choices. Parents play a pivotal role in shaping their children's values and behaviors. By modeling responsible choices in their own lives, parents can inspire their children to follow suit. This not only strengthens the family unit but also empowers the next generation to become responsible global citizens.

In conclusion, valuing responsible choices is of utmost importance for stronger families. By instilling family values centered around sustainability, ethics, and conscious parenting, families can contribute to the betterment of society as a whole. It is our collective responsibility to nurture and preserve the well-being of our families, as they are the bedrock of a sustainable and prosperous future. Let us embrace responsible choices and pave the way for stronger, more resilient families.

Call to action for individuals and families to embrace sustainable consumption

Introduction:
In today's world, where the effects of climate change are becoming increasingly evident, it is crucial for individuals and families to embrace sustainable consumption. By making responsible choices in our everyday lives, we can contribute to a better future for ourselves, our families, and the planet. This subchapter aims to highlight the importance of family values in driving sustainable consumption and provide practical steps for individuals and families to take action.

The Power of Family Values:
Family values play a significant role in shaping our behaviors and attitudes towards consumption. By instilling values such as empathy, responsibility, and environmental consciousness, we can create a culture of sustainable consumption within our families. When we prioritize sustainable choices, we not only reduce our environmental footprint but also set positive examples for future generations.

Take Action:
1. Educate Yourself and Your Family:
Start by educating yourself and your family about the impact of consumption on the environment. Stay informed about sustainable practices and share this knowledge with your loved ones. Teach children the importance of conserving resources, recycling, and reducing waste.

2. Practice Mindful Consumption:
Make mindful choices while purchasing products. Consider the

environmental and social impact of the items you buy. Support local, organic, and fair-trade products whenever possible. Reduce single-use items like plastic bags and water bottles and opt for reusable alternatives.

3.   Reduce   Energy   Usage: Conserve energy by turning off lights and appliances when not in use. Encourage your family to unplug electronic devices when they are fully charged. Use energy-efficient appliances and consider renewable energy sources for your home.

4.   Minimize   Food   Waste: Plan meals in advance to avoid excess food waste. Teach your family to buy only what is necessary and use leftovers creatively. Compost food scraps to reduce landfill waste.

5.   Support   Sustainable   Transportation: Encourage walking, cycling, or using public transportation instead of relying solely on private vehicles. Carpool with friends or neighbors when possible. Consider purchasing fuel-efficient or electric vehicles.

Conclusion:
Embracing sustainable consumption is not only an individual responsibility but also a collective one. By adopting these practices in our daily lives, we can create a significant impact on the environment and inspire others to do the same. Let us prioritize family values and work together towards a sustainable future for ourselves, stronger families, and a healthier planet.